Great Artists
of the World

Claude Monet

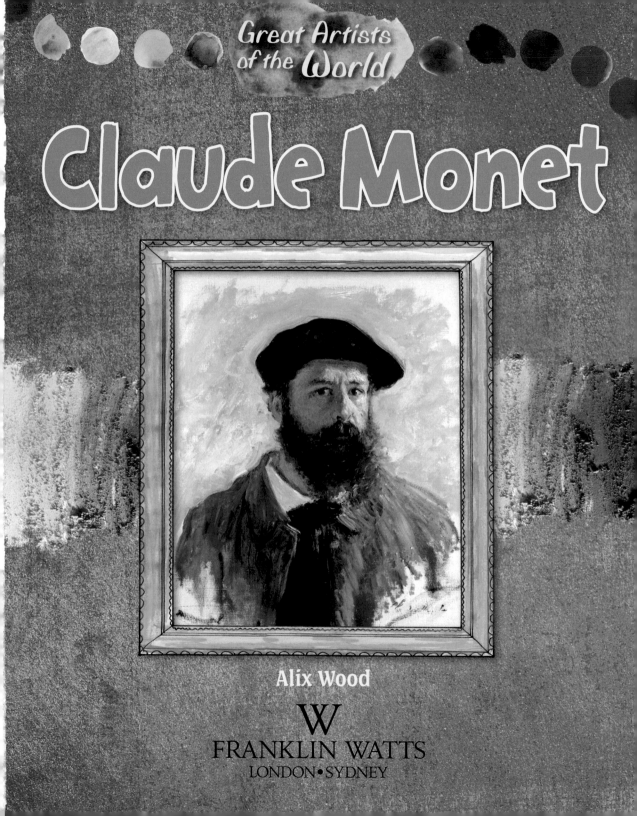

Alix Wood

W
FRANKLIN WATTS
LONDON • SYDNEY

Franklin Watts

First published in Great Britain in 2015 by the Watts Publishing Group

Copyright © Alix Wood Books
Produced for Franklin Watts by Alix Wood Books www.alixwoodbooks.co.uk

Editor: Eloise Macgregor
Designer: Alix Wood

Photo Credits: Cover, 1 ondon / The Brid eman Art Library
4 bottom right © Urban he Met opolitan Museum of Art;
8 © nga; 9 top © nga/ C Collection; 9 bottom © nga; 11 © Blauel/Gnamm -
Artothek; 12 © Peter W rtothek; 13 © Peter Willi - Artothek; © rook76/shutterstock;
17 © The Metropolitan Museum of Art; 18 © Artothek; 21 © Christ 's Images Ltd -
Artothek; 22 top © Chr ie's Images Ltd - Artothek; ter Willi - Artothek;
23 © The Metropolitan nga; 27 © nga/Chest Dale Collection;
28 © Christie's Images L d - Artothek, 3, 4 bo tom left, 5 top, 14, 1 20, 26, 29 © Shutterstock

Northamptonshire Libraries & Information Services NC

Askews & Holts

Dewey number 709

ISBN 978 1 4451 4410 8

Library eBook ISBN 978 1 4451 4411 5

Printed in China

Franklin Watts
An imprint of
Hachette Children's Group
Part of The Watts Publishing Group
Carmelite House
50 Victoria Embankment
London EC4Y 0DZ

An Hachette UK Company

www.hachette.co.uk

www.franklinwatts.co.uk

Contents

Who Was Monet?

Claude Monet was an **Impressionist** painter. He was born in Paris, the second son to his parents, Adolphe and Louise-Justine. His family moved to Le Havre when he was five. Monet's father was a partner in a ship supplies business. His mother was a singer. Monet loved to draw and paint even as a young boy.

Claude Monet

Map of the World

North America

Europe

Asia

Africa

South America

Australia

Le Havre

Le Havre today is a bustling port

Monet didn't really like school. He drew funny pictures of his teachers. He got in trouble for his drawings, but they were very good!

He once said, "School seemed like a prison and I could never bear to stay there, especially when the sunshine beckoned and the sea was smooth".

Young Cartoonist

When Monet was only 11, he studied at the Le Havre school of the arts. He would sell charcoal **caricatures** of local important people for 10 to 20 **francs** each. When young Monet saved 2,000 francs from selling caricatures, he persuaded his father he could make a living from art.

Monet's Aunt

When Monet was 16, his mother died. Monet and his father didn't get along very well. Monet wanted to leave school without graduating. His father was not happy about this. Monet had an aunt, Marie-Jeanne Lecadre. She had no children of her own, and Monet went to live with her.

His aunt was an amateur painter. She let him use her **studio** and encouraged him. At about this time, he met fellow artist Eugène Boudin one day on the beach. Boudin became his **mentor** and persuaded Monet to stop drawing caricatures and to try oil paints instead.

The Garden at Sainte-Adresse, 1867. The garden in this painting is at his aunt's seaside villa. The people sitting down are thought to be Monet's father and his aunt.

Sky and Light

Monet spent two years learning to paint with Eugène Boudin. Boudin painted seascapes of Le Havre and liked to paint in the open air. Boudin thought that an artist should paint from his first impression of a scene. Monet's long career in art was then spent capturing these first impressions.

Boudin took Monet to paint with him outside. In Le Havre there is an amazing light, with rich, blue, cloud-filled skies. The Sun going in and out of the clouds made the landscape dark, then bright, in a flash. Monet and Boudin painted side by side, outside, using portable easels and paint in tubes, trying to catch the light.

Eugène Boudin

The Beach at Villerville, Eugène Boudin, 1864

Sainte-Adresse, Claude Monet, 1867

Big Sky

Boudin often made the sky the main subject of his painting. Can you see his influence in Monet's style?

Monet in Paris

Monet went to Paris in May 1859. His father expected him to go to the School of Fine Art. It was quite an old-fashioned art school. Monet's aunt gave him some money and he went to the Swiss Academy instead. It was cheaper and only had a few hours of classes a week, which suited Monet better.

Claude Monet as a young man

Monet made friends with other painters in Paris named Frédéric Bazille, Auguste Renoir, and Alfred Sisley. They called Monet a '**dandy**' because of the frilly shirts he wore. The friends had no money, and once lived on beans for two whole months!

Village Street in Normandy, painted around 1867. Monet and his friends liked to paint ordinary working people in clear bright colours.

Talented Friends

The friends would paint together, and exhibited at a new art gallery that took paintings the main art gallery had rejected. The painting below by Monet's friend Frédéric Bazille is of Bazille's studio and his friends. You can see the painters Auguste Renoir, Claude Monet and Édouard Manet, the writer Émile Zola and the musician Edmond Maître.

Frédéric Bazille, *The Artist's Studio, Rue de la Condamine, Paris*, 1870.

1: Auguste Renoir   3: Édouard Manet   5: Frédéric Bazille
2: Émile Zola   4: Claude Monet   6: Edmond Maître

A Portrait

The Gaudiberts were a generous, wealthy couple who helped Monet in a bad year. His family had stopped sending him money. He had not sold any paintings and owed lots of money. He was thrown out of his house. The money he got for painting this portrait helped him carry on painting.

Madame Gaudibert, 1868

13

How Monet Painted

Monet only used a few colours when he painted. He never used browns and earth colours and, by 1886, he never used black either. Monet's paint **palette** would have looked like this. Some colours had different names then, because they were made with things we now know are bad for you. For example, titanium white was made of lead then and called lead white.

French ultramarine

emerald green

cobalt blue

viridian green

alizarin crimson

cadmium yellow

vermilion

cadmium yellow light

titanium white

Monet liked to paint the way colours **reflected** in water. Monet even had a floating studio built for him, so he could float on the River Seine and paint. Monet kept paints, brushes, **canvas** and drawing supplies on his boat. He sometimes

Claude Monet in his Studio Boat, 1874, by Édouard Manet

got in a bad mood when his paintings weren't going well. One day he threw all his paints and brushes in the river! The stamp above is of a painting by his friend, Édouard Manet. It shows Monet in his studio boat with his wife, Camille.

A Time in the Army

Monet was selected for National Service and spent a year in North Africa in the army. He became ill with **dysentery** and his aunt managed to get him out of the army. His friend Bazille was not so lucky, and was killed in 1870 fighting in a war.

In London

In July 1870 war broke out between France and Prussia, and Monet fled to London. He liked to paint the haze of **smog** that London had in that period. Monet enjoyed painting the Palace of Westminster, and did, more than a hundred times! He met the artists Charles-François Daubigny and Camille Pissarro while in London. He also met the art dealer Paul Durand-Ruel who sold his paintings for the rest of Monet's life.

Monet once said, *"Durand-Ruel, became for us, our saviour. For more than fifteen years, my painting as well as that of Renoir, Sisley and Pissarro had no other market than through him."*

The Houses of Parliament, Effect of Fog, 1903

Impressionism Is Born

In 1874 several painters including Monet, Renoir and Pissarro held an exhibition of their work. Monet showed five paintings. This small painting below has become one of Monet's most important works, simply because of the title he chose, *Impression, Sunrise*.

Impression, Sunrise,
1872

An art critic said the painting looked "half-finished" like all the works on show, and he called the group "Impressionists". It was meant as an insult!

A Good Salesman

Monet sold his sunrise painting for 800 francs. After this, he often exhibited paintings with a sold sign already on them. This made his paintings seem very desirable and attracted more sales and higher prices.

SOLD

As his paintings began to sell, Monet could afford to take trips abroad. He went to Italy with his friend Renoir. The colours were so different in Italy, Monet had to start using a few new colours on his paint palette. He needed bright turqouise, pinks and oranges. He once said "There are moments when I'm appalled at the colours I'm having to use."

Map showing Italy and France

The House at Giverny

In 1870, Monet married Camille Doncieux. They lived with Ernest and Alice Hoschedé and their six children. Ernest had bought several of Monet's paintings in the past, but had now lost all his money. They moved to a large house in Giverny, in France. Monet loved to paint the house and the beautiful gardens he had made at Giverny.

A Full House

Monet and his wife, Camille, and two children, Jean and Michel, shared the house with Alice and Ernest Hoschedé, and their children, Blanche, Germaine, Suzanne, Marthe, Jean-Pierre and Jacques. Blanche later married Jean Monet. Monet later married Alice, too, after Camille and Ernest had died.

A present-day photograph of Monet's house at Giverny.

The Artist's House at Giverny, 1913

Monet spent many years designing the gardens at his new house. He built a water lily pond with a Japanese bridge over it. He had six gardeners who helped him with his designs. He planted lots of irises. They were his favourite flower.

Haystacks

Before Impressionism, an object was always painted the same basic colour. Oranges were orange and lemons were yellow. Painting outdoors, rather than in a traditional studio, though, meant different light conditions at different times of the day.

Monet loved painting the changing light. He began painting haystacks at different times of day. He started with two canvasses, but as the light changed, he asked his willing helper, his young step-daughter Blanche Hoschedé, to bring him more and more canvasses in a wheelbarrow! Monet would rise before dawn, and paint the first canvas for half an hour.

Haystacks, Morning Effect, 1891

Haystacks at the end of Summer, at Giverny, 1891

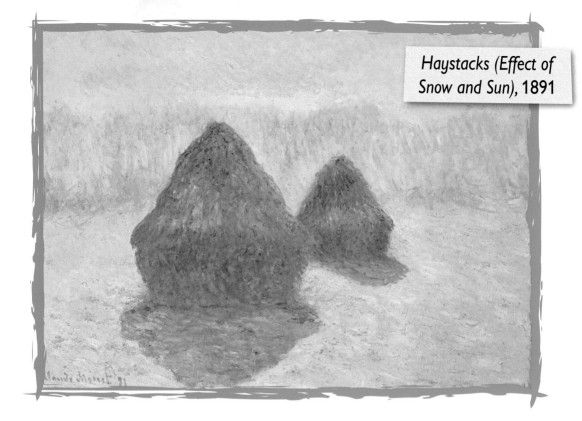

When the light changed, he would switch to the second canvas, and so on. The next day, he would do the same. In each painting, the colour of the haystack is different because the light shining on the haystack is different.

Pulleys and Trenches

Monet loved painting outside so much that when he did a really large painting he had a trench dug in the garden so the canvas could be raised or lowered by pulleys to the right height.

Monet's Garden

Monet now rarely left his garden to paint. He painted hundreds of views of his lily pond. The first paintings of the Japanese bridge at Giverny were quite conventional, like this painting on the right.

Later, Monet started experimenting. He did a series of paintings where his first canvas was painted from up high, looking down at the pond. Then Monet gradually moved down the bank until he was almost at eye level with the water. In the later paintings we can't tell if we are in the lake looking up or on the lake looking down. Filling the canvas, the surface of the pond becomes a world in itself.

The Japanese Footbridge, 1899

Rouen Cathedral

Monet spent three years painting the cathedral at Rouen, in France. He set up in a room with a window overlooking the cathedral. He would work on several canvasses on the same day, like he did when he painted the haystacks. He would change canvasses when the light changed. The cathedral would look misty blue, grey or yellow depending on the weather and the light.

Changing Light

These two photographs are of the front of Rouen cathedral as it looks today. If you look at the trees in the background you can see they are taken at the same time of year — probably the same day — but the cathedral looks so different. Imagine if you started painting the top one and the light changed this much. You'd have to go back and start again!

Rouen Cathedral, West Façade, Sunlight, 1894

Monet's Last Paintings

As Monet got older he began to lose his eyesight. **Cataracts** made his eyes see colours differently and made things blurry. Whites and greens now looked yellow, and reds became oranges. Blues and purples looked like red and yellow to him. Monet went on painting. He knew what colour he was using by the labels on the tubes and the order he put them on his palette.

The Japanese Bridge, around 1920

The painting on the left is of the same bridge as on page 25. It looks very different. It was done when Monet's eyes were at their worst. After a while the cataracts got so bad he was unable to paint. He had an operation which helped one eye to see.

Some of the last paintings Monet did were a series of enormous water lily murals. He built a special studio to paint them in. He painted them from memory. Over 2 m high and up to 17 m long, they now hang in the Musée de l'Orangerie in Paris.

No Black for Monet

Monet died at the age of 86, at home in his bed. As Monet always avoided black in his painting, when he died his friend Georges Clemenceau didn't like the black sheet covering the coffin. He shouted : "No! No black for Monet!" and replaced it with a flowered cover.

The house and gardens at Giverny are now a museum

Glossary

canvas
A piece of cloth used as a surface for painting.

caricatures
Drawings that exaggerate a person's features for comic effect.

cataracts
Clouding of the lens of the eyes.

dandy
A man who is very interested in his clothing and appearance.

dysentery
A painful illness of the intestine, with diarrhoea, and often a fever.

francs
The old unit of money of France and Belgium.

Impressionist
An artist who concentrates on painting the impression of a scene using unmixed primary colours and small brush strokes to simulate light.

palette
A board used by a painter to mix paints on.

mentor
A wise and trusted teacher.

reflected
Light that is bent or thrown back.

smog
A thick haze caused by sunlight on air polluted by smoke and fumes.

studio
The working place of an artist.

Websites

A Pinterest site showing fun Monet project ideas
https://uk.pinterest.com/patty_palmer2/claude-monet-art-project-for-kids/

A simple website showing all the artist's work
http://www.claudemonetgallery.org

Every effort has been made by the publisher to ensure that these websites contain no inappropriate or offensive material. However, because of the nature of the Internet, it is impossible to guarantee that the content of these sites will not be altered. We strongly advise that Internet access is supervised by a responsible adult.

Read More

Mayhew, James. *Katie and the Waterlily Pond: A Journey Through Five Magical Monet Masterpieces*. Lives of the Artists. London, UK: Orchard Books, 2011.

Anholt, Laurence. *The Magical Garden of Claude Monet* (Anholt's Artists). London, UK: Frances Lincoln, 1997.

Venezia, Mike. *Claude Monet* (Getting to Know the World's Greatest Artists) revised edition. London, UK: Franklin Watts, 2014.

Index